A+ books

Awesome
African
Animals!

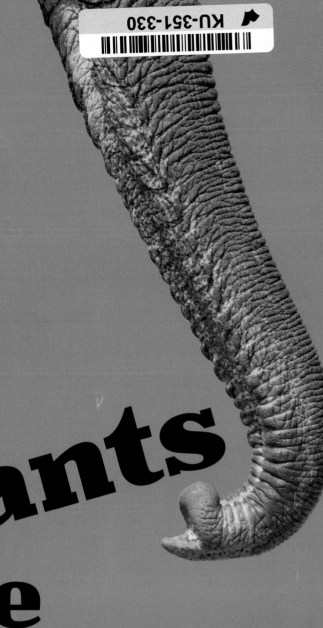

Elephants Are Awesome!

by Martha E. H. Rustad

Consultant: Jackie Gai, DVM
Captive Wildlife Vet

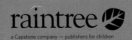
raintree
a Capstone company — publishers for children

Raintree is an imprint of Capstone Global Library Limited, a company incorporated in England and Wales having its registered office at 7 Pilgrim Street, London, EC4V 6LB – Registered company number: 6695582

www.raintree.co.uk
myorders@raintree.co.uk

Text © Capstone Global Library Limited 2015

Edited by Mari Bolte and Erika Shores
Designed by Cynthia Della-Rovere
Picture research by Svetlana Zhurkin
Production by Morgan Walters
Printed and bound in China by Nordica.
0914/CA21401520

For Mac, Marit, and Nash. —MEHR

ISBN 978-1-406-28845-2
18 17 16 15 14
10 9 8 7 6 5 4 3 2 1

British Library Cataloguing in Publication Data
A full catalogue record for this book is available from the British Library.

Acknowledgements
We would like to thank the following for permission to reproduce photographs: iStockphotos: Serge_Vero, 24—25; Newscom: Ingram Publishing, 27 (bottom); Shutterstock: Alexander Kuguchin, 4 (bottom), Amy Nichole Harris, 5, Andre Klopper, 22 (top), BGSmith, cover (top), Black Sheep Media (grass), back cover and throughout, Chris Erasmus, 22 (bottom), Costas Anton Dumitrescu, 20—21, Donovan van Staden, 9, Eric Isselee, back cover, 13, 15 (top), 32, Four Oaks, 10 (left), 12, 23, Gerrit_de_Vries, 18 (bottom), Hector Conesa, cover (bottom), Jez Bennett, 10—11, Konstantin Goldenberg, 14, Marie-Anne Aberson, 19, Mark Bridger, 15 (bottom), Matej Hudovernik, 26, moizhusein, 6—7, Nobby Clarke, 21 (top), NREY, 24 (top), Peter Betts, 27 (top), Photo Love, cover (middle), 1, 11 (right), PlusONE, 4 (top), Richard Peterson, 8, Steffen Foerster, 28—29, Tobie Oosthuizen, 16, Villiers Steyn, 17, 18 (top)

We would like to thank Jackie Gai, DVM, for her invaluable help in the preparation of this book.

Contents

Elephants at home

Rumble, rumble! The savannah ground shakes. A herd of African elephants thunders by.

These elephants make their homes in many African habitats. They travel from savannahs to forests to mountains. They roam from deserts to swamps.

Just keep walking! Elephants migrate across Africa. Strong, solid legs carry their heavy grey bodies. They look for food and water

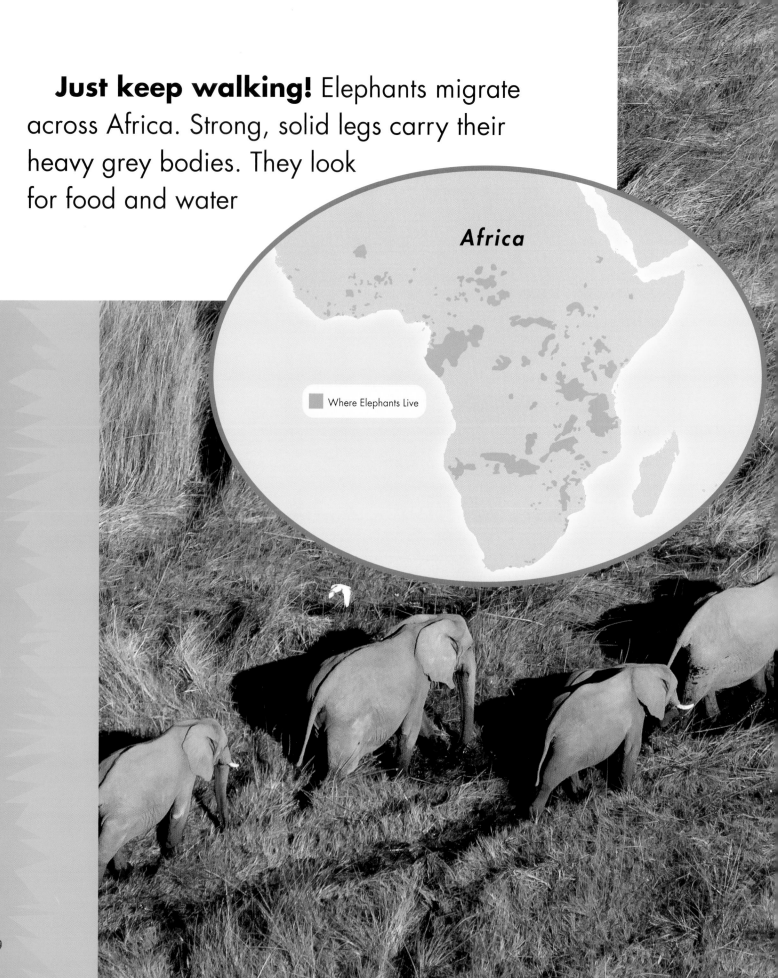

Africa

Where Elephants Live

Elephants travel hundreds of kilometres each year. They walk about 8 kilometres (5 miles) per hour. In short bursts, elephants can reach speeds of 40 kilometres (25 miles) per hour.

African elephants are the biggest animals on land. They are larger than Asian elephants. In fact, elephants never never stop growing! They can weigh as much as 7 tonnes. That is almost as much as a bus.

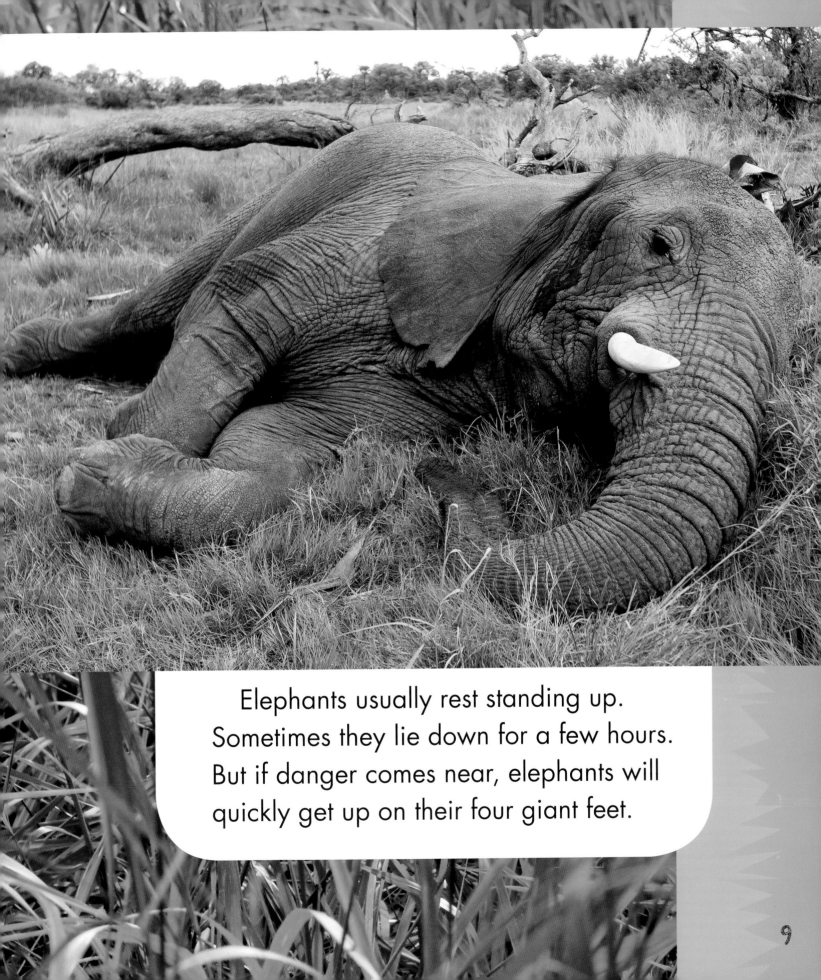

Elephants usually rest standing up. Sometimes they lie down for a few hours. But if danger comes near, elephants will quickly get up on their four giant feet.

From trunk to tail

Sniff! Elephants lift up their trunks to smell. They also breathe through this long nose.

Two tips on the end of a trunk work like fingers. Elephants use their trunks to grab leaves from branches. Their strong trunks pull trees from the ground.

Dig! Tusks are helpful tools. Elephants use tusks to dig holes to find water. Tusks help them peel bark from trees. Tusks are also used for fighting.

Elephants use their ears to do more than listen. Large ears help elephants to stay cool. Blood flows through their thin ears. Elephants flap their ears to cool the blood. **Thwap!**

Grab my tail! There is a tuft of hair at the end of an elephant's tail. A very young elephant calf can hold an adult's tail with its trunk.

Hungry, thirsty and hot

Chomp, chomp! Enormous elephants eat and eat. They spend all day eating to fuel their big bodies. An adult male elephant eats up to 180 kilograms (400 pounds) of food each day.

Elephants munch plants and grasses. They gobble fruit and seeds. Their four wide, flat molars chew and chew.

Slurp! Hot, thirsty elephants drink lots of water. Adults drink up to 190 litres (50 gallons) every day.

Squirt! Elephant trunks suck up water like a straw. Then the elephants shoot water into their mouths.

Spray! Elephants spray water on their bodies to cool off. They sprinkle dirt and mud on their wrinkled skin. It works like sunscreen.

Elephant families

Follow me! The oldest female in the family is called a matriarch. She leads her sisters, her daughters and their calves. The matriarch remembers where to find food and water for her family.

Groups of families are called herds.
Herds gather at watering holes. Elephants
touch and twist trunks to say hello.

Squeak! A hungry calf drinks milk from its mother. Calves look like small adults. The whole family cares for the calves. They teach them, play with them and keep them safe.

Male elephants leave their family when they are around 10 years old. Groups of young males sometimes live together. But many male elephants live alone. Females stay with their family for life. Elephants live for up to 70 years.

Staying safe

Trumpet! Elephants warn each other of danger. Only a few predators try to attack elephants. But elephants watch out for lions, crocodiles and hyenas. An elephant family forms a circle. They keep young and sick elephants safe.

Humans are the biggest danger to elephants. Humans build homes in the paths where elephants travel. Elephants have fewer safe places to live. Some hunters kill elephants for their ivory tusks.

Look! Take a picture! Tourists visit reserves to see elephants in their natural habitats. Humans can help elephants by saving the habitat of these awesome African animals.

Glossary

calf young elephant

fuel give a person or thing energy to work and be active

habitat place where an animal or plant naturally lives

ivory hard, creamy-white material of an animal's tusk

matriarch female leader of a group or herd

migrate move from one place to another when seasons change or to look for food

molar wide tooth used to chew food

predator animal that hunts other animals for food

reserve area of land kept for a special purpose such as protecting plants and animals

savannah flat, grassy area of land with few or no trees

tourist person who is travelling or on holiday abroad

trunk elephant's long nose and upper lip

tusk very long, pointed tooth that sticks out of the mouth

Books

Amazing Elephants (Walk on the Wild Side), Charlotte Guillain (Raintree, 2013)

Elephant (Animal Diaries), Steve Parker (QEB Publishing, 2012)

Websites

http://kids.nationalgeographic.com/animals/african-elephant/
Full of fun facts and trivia about African elephants.

**http://gowild.wwf.org.uk/regions/africa-fact-files/
african-elephant**
Hear an African elephant! Find out more about this amazing animal. Read stories about African animals and have a go at some fun activities.

Comprehension questions

1. Look at the picture on pages 24–25. Describe what you see in the picture. Then read the text.

2. Why do elephants need to travel so far to find food and water?

3. Describe the dangers an elephant faces every day.

Index